Common Core Lessons & Activities:
Map Skills

By Carole Marsh
Published by Gallopade International, Inc.
©Carole Marsh/Gallopade
Printed in the U.S.A. (Peachtree City, Georgia)

TABLE OF CONTENTS

What Are Maps?: Reading Informational Text 2
Cartography: Main Idea 3
Reading a Map: Applying Concepts 4
A Community Map: Map Activity 6
Using a Simple Grid: Concepts & Processes **G** 8
Imaginary Lines Divide the Earth: Reading Informational Text 10
Views of the World: Comparison of Primary Sources 11
Building a Map: Concepts & Processes **G** 12
Relative & Absolute Location: Applying Concepts 14
Location, Location, Location: Classifying Information 16
Political & Climate Maps: Compare & Contrast **GO**[1] 18
Physical & Resource Maps: Comparison of Sources 20
A Map Series: Graphical Data Analysis 22
Aerial Painting: Primary Source Analysis 23
Common Core Correlations 24

G: Includes Graphic Organizer
GO: Graphic Organizer is also available 8½" x 11" online
download at www.gallopade.com/client/go
(numbers above correspond to the graphic organizer numbers online)

READING INFORMATIONAL TEXT

What Are Maps?

Read the text and answer the questions.

Maps are some of the most useful tools for studying geography. Maps are representations of the Earth's surface. Maps typically show a view from above the ground. Maps can be drawings, paintings, photographs, diagrams, or globes—anything that shows what an area (land and water) looks like. Maps might show a city, state, country, or even the whole Earth! To fit on a page, locations and objects on a map are drawn in smaller scale.

Maps include important information about an area. A map might show the locations of landforms like mountains, plains, lakes, rivers, oceans, and more. Maps can show the locations of man-made structures like roads, bridges, and buildings. Maps can show borders between cities, states, and countries. Some maps use lines and colors to show patterns of elevation, rainfall, or temperature. Because most maps are flat, they cannot show everything about an area. Mapmakers must choose which information to show.

Some people say that a picture is worth a thousand words. That is definitely true for a map. Maps provide a clear picture of an area without having to describe every detail in words. Maps can show us how an area looks today, in the past, or how things have changed over time. Historical maps can even give us clues about who made them, what the world was like at the time, and what people thought was important.

1. Match the following questions to whether they would be best answered by paragraph 1, 2, or 3 of the text.
   A. _____ What information do maps contain?
   B. _____ Why should you study maps?
   C. _____ What is a map?

2. Explain what is meant by the statement, "a map shows a view from above the ground." Why is this an important point?

3. List three types of information that might be included on a map.

4. A. Explain the meaning of "A picture is worth a thousand words."
   B. Why might this be true for a map? Cite evidence from the text to support your answer.

©Carole Marsh/Gallopade • www.gallopade.com • page 2

MAIN IDEA

Cartography

Read the text and answer the questions.

The science of mapmaking is called <u>cartography</u>. A person who makes maps is called a <u>cartographer</u>. The science of cartography began with simple drawings and has improved greatly because of the technology we have today.

Cartography is one of the oldest sciences. The earliest maps were simple drawings scratched in clay by the ancient people of Mesopotamia. Ancient Greeks, ancient Romans, and ancient Egyptians also drew simple maps using brushes and paper to show the location of important places and landmarks.

Early cartographers used the position of the stars to measure distances on the Earth. Observation tools such as the sextant and telescope improved their ability to map accurately. The invention of the compass also helped to improve the accuracy of mapping directions. Cartographers used the compass to better describe objects as being located north, south, east, or west. The invention of the printing press allowed maps to be copied and sold in large numbers to many different explorers, merchants, and sailors.

Mapmaking today is much more accurate than it was in the past. Cartographers gather precise data from satellites that digitally map the Earth's surface and record information. Global positioning satellites (GPS) can give an exact location of any object or place on the Earth. Most cartographers today produce maps using computer software and digital maps. Many maps are available online. Some maps today are even interactive, which allows the user to choose which data is displayed for an area.

1. A. What is the main idea of this text?
   B. List at least three supporting details from the text that support the main idea.

2. A. What is a synonym for <u>cartography</u> as it is used in the text?
   B. A person who makes a map is called a _____.

3. A. What did ancient civilizations use to make maps?
   B. What improvements were made to the earliest maps?
   C. How has cartography changed due to recent technology?

APPLYING CONCEPTS
Reading a Map

Read the text and answer the questions.

To understand what information a map contains, you must know how to read one. Fortunately, maps have many features that explain how we should read them.

Title and Author
Most maps contain a title. A map's title is often located at the top of the map, or sometimes in a separate box to the side or bottom. A map's title often gives important information about the map, such as what area the map is showing, when the map was created, or what themes the map represents.

Some maps might include the name of the author. A map might be made by one author, a group of people, or a whole organization. Knowing who made the map can give you clues to the purpose of the map. For example, if the map was made by the U.S. Department of Agriculture, you might assume that the map contains information about farmland or the environment. You also know that the map contains information about areas of the United States and might be especially useful to farmers.

Compass Rose
A map typically includes a <u>compass rose</u>. A compass rose shows the cardinal directions of north, south, east, and west. A compass rose also shows intermediate directions—northeast, northwest, southeast, and southwest.

Symbols, Map Key, and Scale
Most maps have <u>symbols</u>. Symbols show the location of natural objects such as landforms and man-made objects such as cities, roads, bridges, and buildings. However, symbols can represent anything of importance on a map. But, how do you know what each symbol represents? Maps usually include a <u>map key</u>, or <u>legend</u>, that explains what each symbol means.

Because a map is a smaller representation of a much, much larger area, cartographers include a <u>scale</u>. Scales are measurements that compare real distances to the distances on a much smaller map. One inch on a map could represent 100 miles of real-life distance.

PART A: Use information from the text to answer the questions.

1. A. List the important features of a map.
   B. What is the purpose of including map features?
2. Which map features would be useful for giving directions?
3. Which map features give information about who made the map or why the map was made?
4. Which map features would be useful for locating objects on a map? Explain why.

PART B: Look at the map and use what you learned from the text to answer the questions.

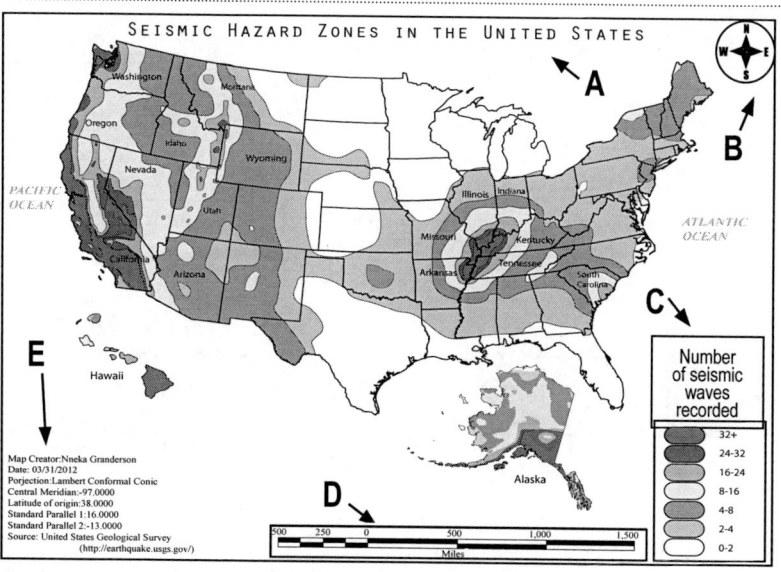

SEISMIC HAZARD ZONES IN THE UNITED STATES

* Seismic waves are vibrations in the Earth due to earthquake activity.

5. Identify each map feature marked A, B, C, D, and E.
   A. _____
   B. _____
   C. _____
   D. _____
   E. _____

6. A. What area of land is shown by this map?
   B. What map feature tells you this information?

7. Who might be interested in viewing this type of map? Explain.

©Carole Marsh/Gallopade • www.gallopade.com • page 5

MAP ACTIVITY

A Community Map

Look at the map and answer the questions.

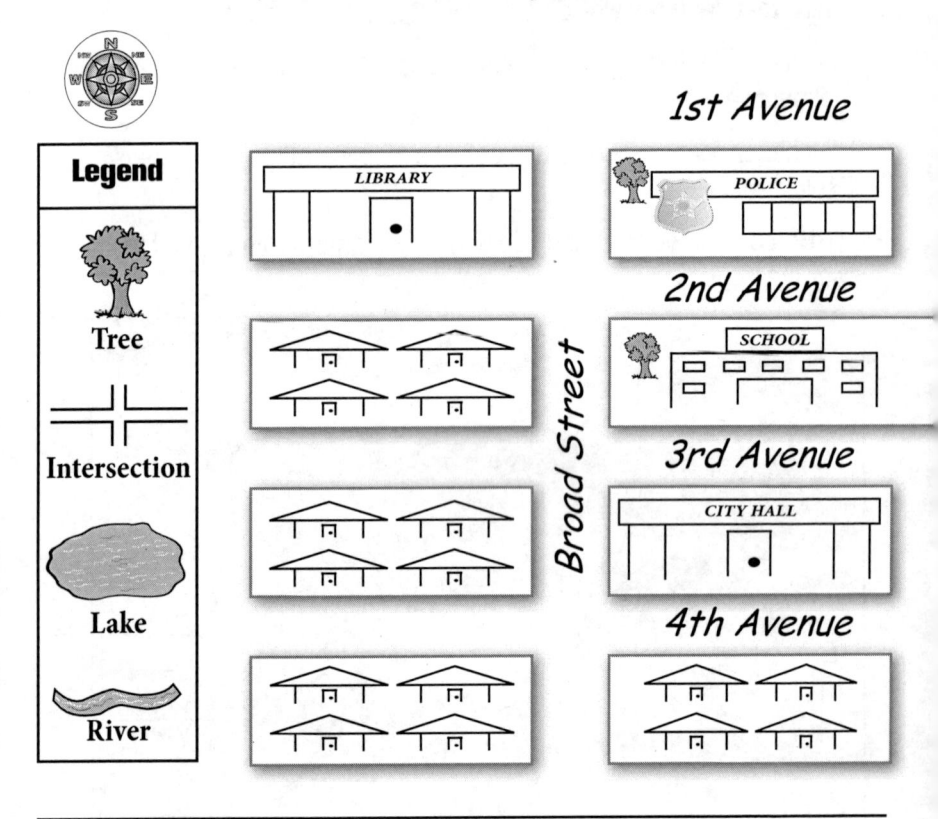

1. A. What is the title of this map?
   B. What information can you draw from this map's title?
2. A. Locate the map legend on the community map.
   B. What types of information does it provide?
3. Look at the buildings in this community. What can you infer about the types of jobs people do in this community?
4. A. Locate the compass rose.
   B. How might this help you if you needed to give directions?
5. Imagine you are giving directions to a friend. Describe how to get to your home from your school. Will this task be easier if you drew a map like the one above? Why or why not?

Miller Community Map

[Map showing: Hospital, Grocery Store, Ice Cream, Shopping Mall, Pizza on Fuller Ave; Miller Park Road running north-south; Miller Park with lake and trees; forest area. A building (unlabeled) sits between Ice Cream and Shopping Mall.]

6. Follow the directions below and draw the route on the map.
   a) First, start at the library.
   b) Then, go south on Broad Street.
   c) Turn east on 4th Avenue.
   d) Continue on 4th Avenue past City Hall and the Shopping Mall.
   e) When you see a forest to the South, stop and turn North.
   Where are you?

7. Imagine a visitor at City Hall wants to get to the Grocery Store. Step by step, use the map to write a list of directions from City Hall to the Grocery Store. Include street names, cardinal directions, and which landmarks he/she will see along the way.

©Carole Marsh/Gallopade • www.gallopade.com • page 7

CONCEPTS & PROCESSES

Using a Simple Grid

Read the text, look at the map, and answer the questions.

Every place on the Earth has a location! To easily find and describe locations on the Earth's surface, cartographers draw imaginary lines that intersect on the map to create a <u>grid</u>. Grids help show location. The simplest grid is an alphanumeric grid.

How to read an alphanumeric grid
An alphanumeric grid uses letters and numbers. "Alpha" refers to letters of the alphabet (A, B, C, ...), and "numeric" refers to numbers (1, 2, 3, ...). Each square of the grid is named by its corresponding letter and number. You can read the grid by locating the letter of the square and then the number.

This combination of letters and numbers is one way to describe location on a map. Objects in the top left square of the grid are said to be at location A1.

PART A: Use the text to answer these questions.

1. What is the purpose of drawing a grid on a map?
2. Describe what an "alphanumeric" grid is.
3. Explain why the text describes the grid lines on a map as "imaginary."
4. Use what you learned from the text to fill in the names of each square in the alphanumeric grid below. A few squares have been completed as examples.

	1	2	3	4	5
A	A1				
B				B4	
C					
D		D2			

©Carole Marsh/Gallopade • www.gallopade.com • page 8

STATE OF MISSISSIPPI

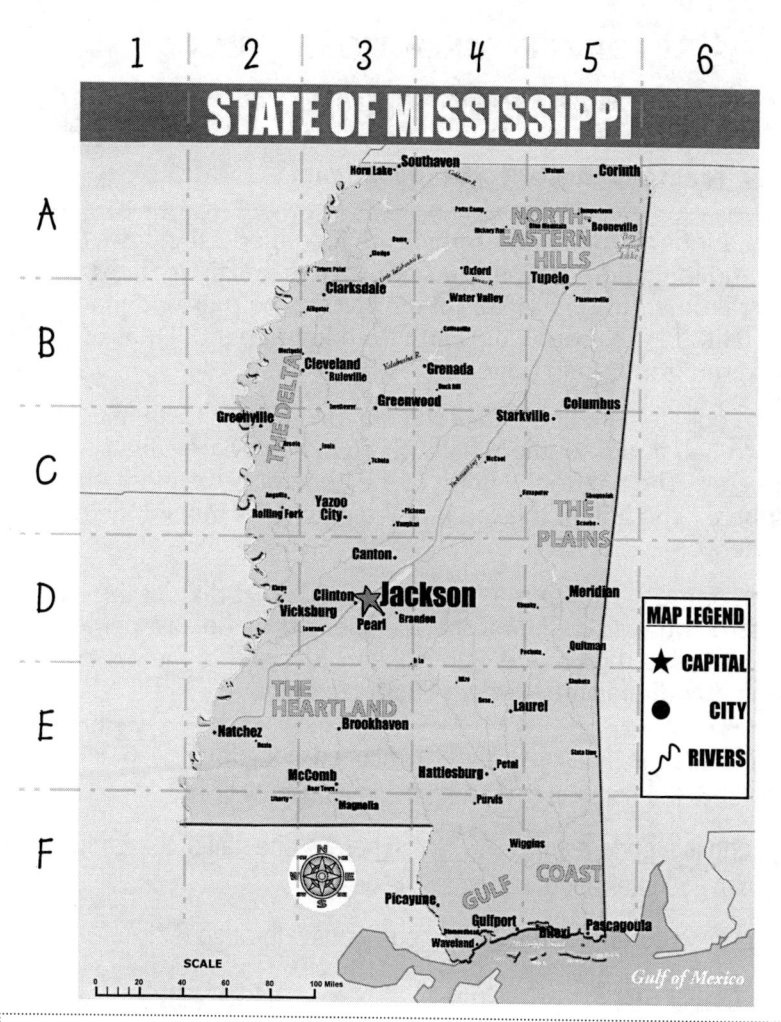

PART B: Use the text and the map to answer these questions.

5. What does the title tell you about the map?
6. Locate the map legend. What types of information are shown?
7. Use the alphanumeric grid to locate each of the following cities. One has been completed as an example.
   A. __D5__ Meridian   D. _____ Natchez
   B. _____ Jackson   E. _____ Picayune
   C. _____ Starkville   F. _____ Clarksdale
8. The Northeastern Hills are found in which squares of the grid?
9. The Heartland is primarily located in which squares of the grid?

©Carole Marsh/Gallopade • www.gallopade.com • page 9

READING INFORMATIONAL TEXT
Imaginary Lines Divide the Earth

Read the text and answer the questions.

> Locations on the Earth's surface are identified using lines of latitude and longitude. Mapmakers draw these imaginary lines, and several other lines, on maps of the Earth to help us find places. Lines of latitude run around the Earth from left to right. Lines of longitude run from top to bottom.
>
> The <u>equator</u> is a line of latitude that divides the Earth into a northern half and a southern half. The two halves are called <u>hemispheres</u>. The half to the north of the equator is the Northern Hemisphere. The half to the south of the equator is the Southern Hemisphere.
>
> The <u>prime meridian</u> is a line of longitude that divides the Earth into eastern and western hemispheres. The half to the east of the prime meridian is the Eastern Hemisphere. The half to the west of the prime meridian is the Western Hemisphere.

1. A. What are the "imaginary lines" mentioned in the text?
   B. What is the purpose of drawing these imaginary lines?

2. The Earth is a sphere shape. A <u>hemisphere</u> is one half of the Earth. What can you infer about the prefix "hemi"?

3. Look at the diagrams and complete questions A through F.

Diagram 1   **Diagram 2**

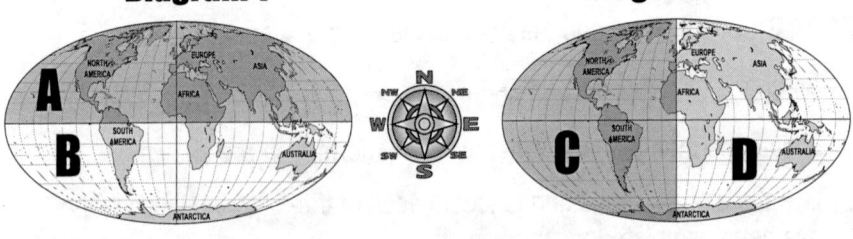

A. Use the text to label the <u>equator</u> on Diagram 1.
B. Use the text to identify the <u>prime meridian</u> on Diagram 2.
C. What hemisphere is represented by the section labeled A?
D. What hemisphere is represented by the section labeled B?
E. What hemisphere is represented by the section labeled C?
F. What hemisphere is represented by the section labeled D?

COMPARISON OF PRIMARY SOURCES
Views of the World

Look at the maps and answer the questions.

A Map of the Entire World and Corrected with Other Lands of Amerigo Vespucci (Martin Waldseemuller 1507)

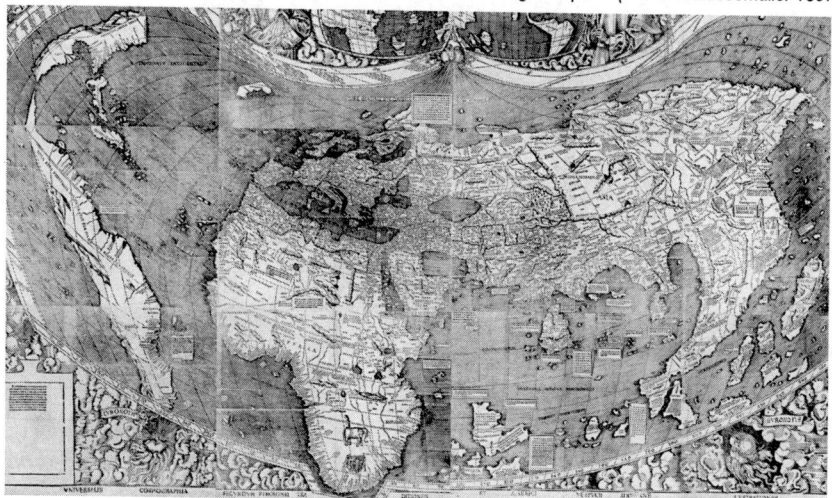

A Modern and Completely Correct Map of the Entire World (Joan Blaeu, 1659)

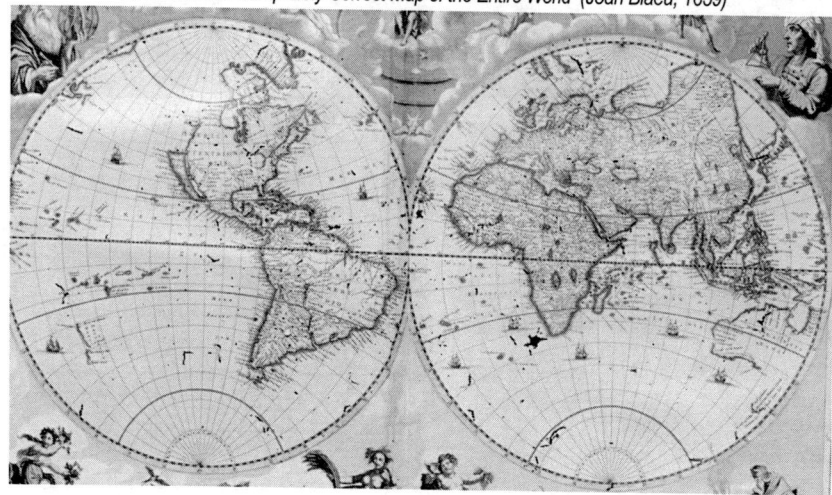

1. List at least 5 similarities and 5 differences between the two sources.
2. A. Explain why the first map's title is not an accurate description.
   B. What information was not available at the time of its creation?
3. A. Describe the layout of the second map.
   B. Why might the author have chosen to show the Earth this way?

CONCEPTS & PROCESSES

Building a Map

Look at the series of steps in this mapmaking process. Explain what map feature(s) is/are being added in each step of the mapmaking process.

Explain why each map feature is important, and draw conclusions about why the mapmaker chose to include that feature at that particular step in the process.

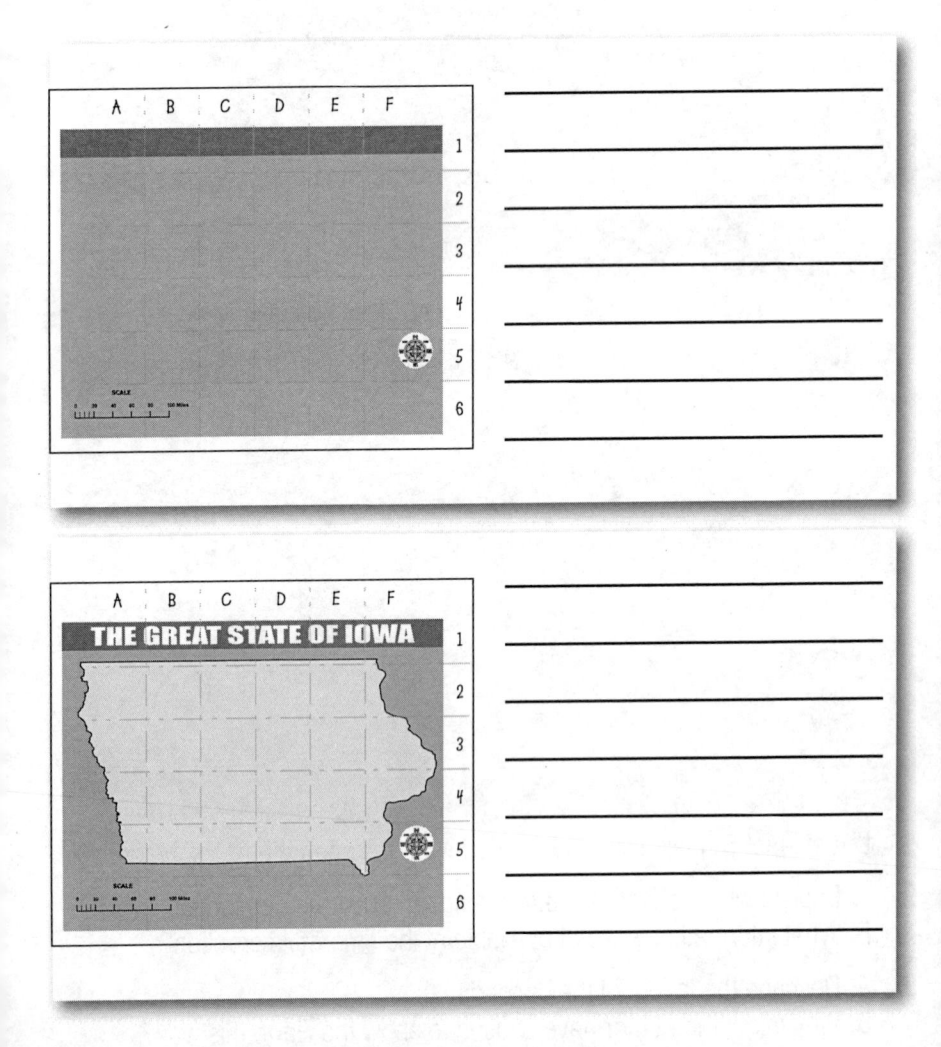

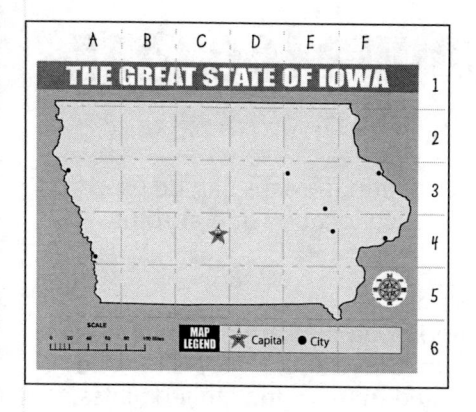

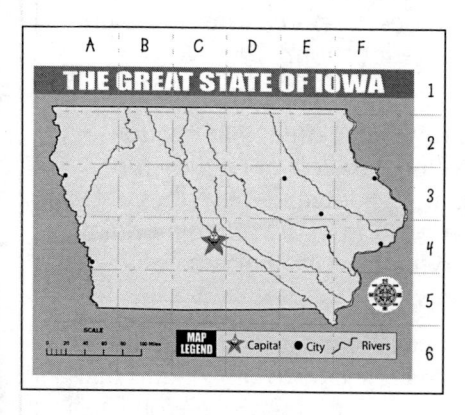

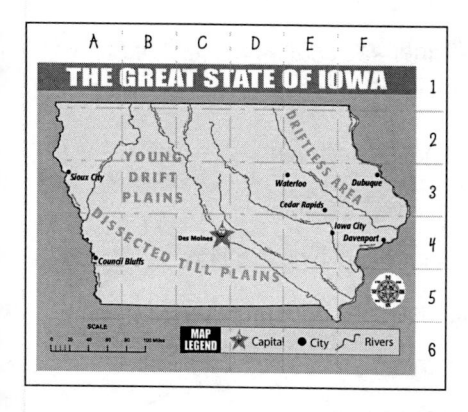

©Carole Marsh/Gallopade • www.gallopade.com • page 13

APPLYING CONCEPTS

Relative & Absolute Location

Read the text and answer the questions.

Every place on the Earth has a location! Maps can be used to describe location in two ways—relative location and absolute location.

Relative Location

Relative location describes a point on the Earth by comparing it with another location. For example, Cleveland, Ohio, is located east of Toledo, Ohio. Canada is located north of the United States. Those are both relative locations.

Relative location is very useful for explaining and describing location, but it is not an exact way to describe location. To describe exact location, it is best to use absolute location.

Latitude and Longitude: A Grid for Absolute Location

Latitude describes a position on Earth's surface in relation to the equator. Imaginary circles called parallels of latitude run around the Earth parallel to the equator. Longitude describes a point's position on Earth's surface in relation to the prime meridian. Meridians of longitude are imaginary half circles that run between the geographic North and South Poles.

The lines of latitude and longitude form a grid around the Earth. The intersection of these lines creates a coordinate grid that can be used to describe the absolute location of any place on Earth. Cartographers use this grid to locate the exact position of places on the Earth's surface.

PART A: Use the text to determine whether each statement is **true (T)** or **false (F)**. Rewrite each false statement to be true.

1. _____ Some places on Earth do not have a location.

2. _____ Absolute locations describe an exact location.

3. _____ Relative location is not helpful for describing location.

4. _____ Intersecting latitude and longitude lines on a map form a grid.

5. _____ Relative location is more accurate than absolute location.

6. _____ Lines of latitude are based on the equator.

PART B: Read the text, look at the map, and answer the questions.

Latitude and longitude as coordinates

Absolute locations are usually measured in degrees (°) latitude and longitude. Latitude is measured North from the equator by degrees North (°N) and south from the equator by degrees South (°S). Similarly, longitude is measured from the prime meridian by degrees East (°E) and degrees West (°W).

Any point on the Earth's surface can be measured using a combination of latitude and longitude. Latitude and longitude are written as coordinates (°Latitude, °Longitude). For example, in the map below, Miami is approximately 25°N latitude and 80°W longitude—(25°N, 80°W).

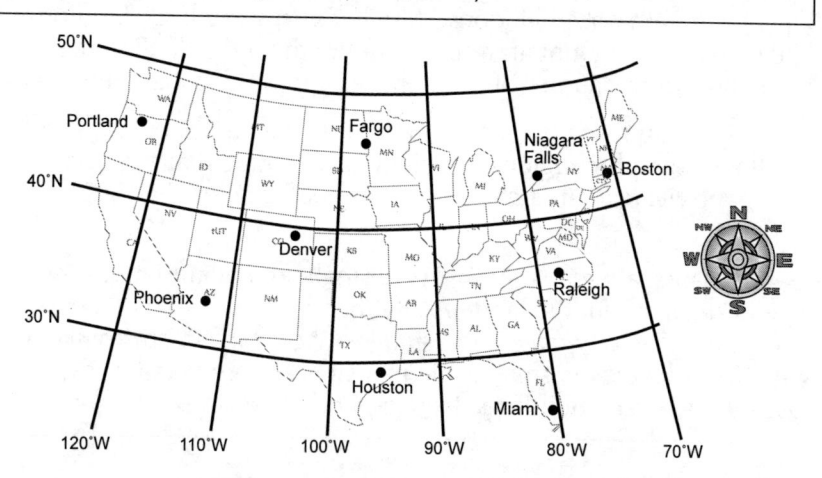

7. What are the benefits of using a grid to describe location?

8. A. Which part of the coordinate (45°S, 54°E) indicates latitude?
   B. Which part of the coordinate (45°S, 54°E) indicates longitude?

9. Use the map to identify what is located at each of the following latitude and longitude coordinates.
   A. (43°N, 71°W) _____
   B. (39°N, 104°W) _____
   C. (29°N, 95°W) _____
   D. (46°N, 97°W) _____

10. Make inferences based on what you have learned to answer the questions.
    A. Is the United States in the Northern or Southern Hemisphere?
    B. Is the United States in the Eastern or Western Hemisphere?
    C. How do you know?

CLASSIFYING INFORMATION

Location, Location, Location

Read the text and answer Parts A and B.

The Earth's surface is very wide. However, any location on the Earth can be mapped using different scales. Some maps show large areas of the Earth, and some maps show small areas.

A large-scale map shows a vast area of land, but shows less detail about the land. A large-scale map might feature a state, country or even the whole globe. A large-scale map might display large cities, but not small ones. It might also show large landforms like oceans and mountain ranges, but not the individual names of mountains or the names of smaller seas and other geographic areas.

A medium-scale map might include the names of states and smaller geographic regions. It might also include major mountains, lakes, and rivers in an area, or the names of smaller cities and towns.

Small-scale maps show a very small area of land, but show greater detail about the land. A city map is an example of a small-scale map. The city map is too small to show large features like a state map. However, small-scale maps have more detail, showing roads, hills, rivers, buildings, bridges, and other objects.

PART A: Use the text to determine whether each of the statements is **true (T)** or **false (F)**. Rewrite each false statement to be true.

1. ____ The scale of a map can be changed to show more or less land area.

2. ____ Small-scale maps contain the most detailed and accurate descriptions of an area of land.

3. ____ Scale is a measurement of distance on a map. The larger the scale the greater the distance the map covers.

4. ____ A map of Europe would most likely be drawn on a medium-scale map.

5. ____ A community map would be drawn on a large-scale map.

6. ____ A small-scale map typically includes only smaller landforms.

PART B: Look at the maps and answer the questions.

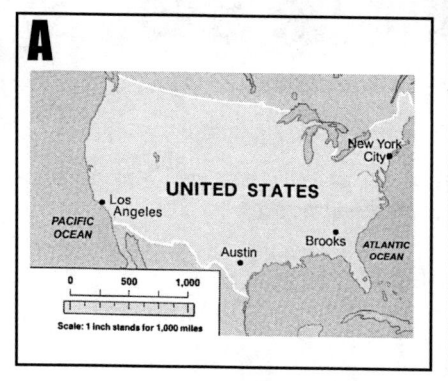

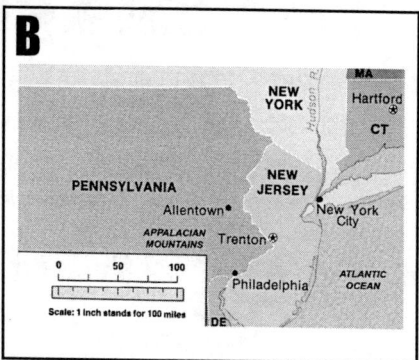

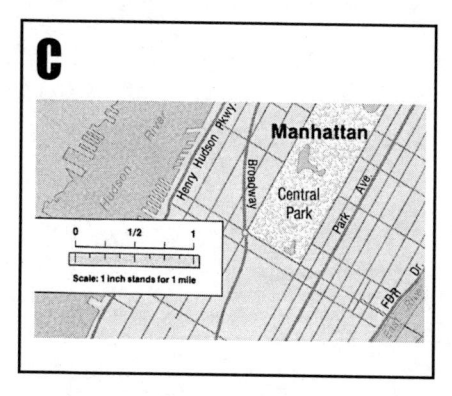

A — United States map showing Los Angeles, Austin, Brooks, New York City, Pacific Ocean, Atlantic Ocean. Scale: 1 inch stands for 1,000 miles.

B — Regional map showing Pennsylvania, New Jersey, New York, Connecticut, Massachusetts, with Allentown, Trenton, Philadelphia, Hartford, New York City, Appalachian Mountains, Hudson R., Atlantic Ocean, DE. Scale: 1 inch stands for 100 miles.

C — Manhattan map showing Hudson River, Henry Hudson Pkwy., Broadway, Central Park, Park Ave., FDR Dr. Scale: 1 inch stands for 1 mile.

7. A. What types of information are shown in each map?
   B. How are all three similar? How are all three different?

8. A. Which map represents a small-scale map—A, B, or C?
   B. Which map represents a medium-scale map—A, B, or C?
   C. Which map represents a large-scale map—A, B, or C?

9. A. Which map shows New York City's location within the U.S.?
   B. Which map shows New York City and its neighboring states?
   C Which map shows a small section of New York City?

10. What units of measurement are used to scale each map? Explain why.

11. Looking at all three maps gives us much more information about New York City than looking at just one map individually.
    A. What information would be lost if map A were not available?
    B. What information would be lost if map B were not available?
    C. What information would be lost if map C were not available?

COMPARE & CONTRAST

Political & Climate Maps

Look at both maps and answer the questions.

Political maps show country and state boundaries, capitals, and major cities.

Climate maps show general patterns of climate and precipitation in an area. Cartographers use colors or patterns to show different climate or precipitation zones.

A Political Map of the United States

1. What information can you gather about the map from its title?
2. A. Is this map a large-scale map or a small-scale map? Explain.
   B. What extra information is included about the United States, but not about Canada or Mexico?
3. Explain why a compass rose is included on the map.
4. Describe the relative location of the United States in relation to Mexico and Canada.
5. Describe the relative location of the United States to the Atlantic Ocean and Pacific Ocean.
6. Infer why the mapmaker did not include small political boundaries like district lines and county lines in each state.

Climates of North America

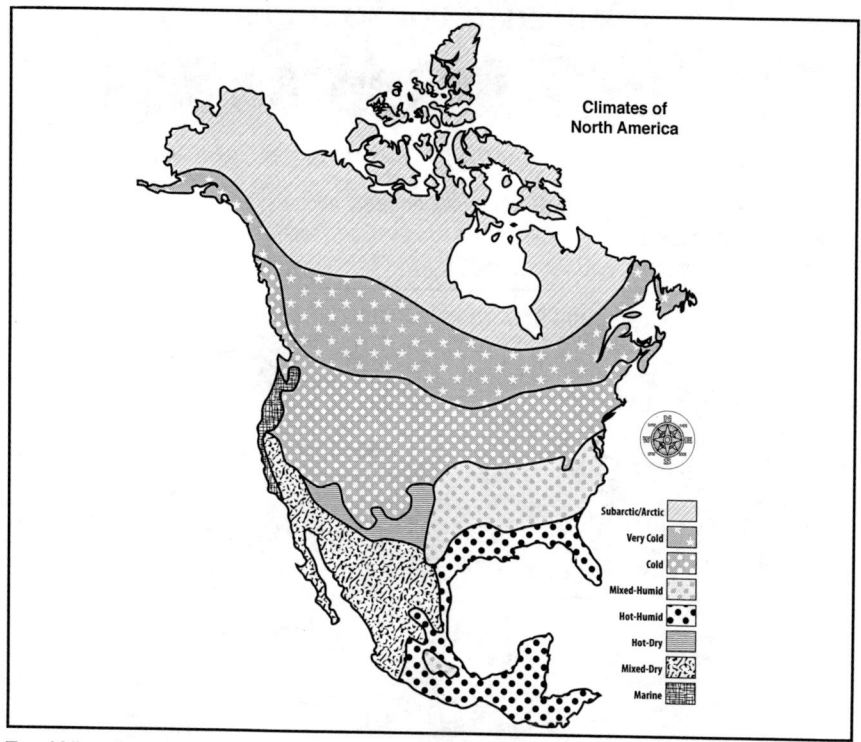

Key:
- Subarctic/Arctic
- Very Cold
- Cold
- Mixed-Humid
- Hot-Humid
- Hot-Dry
- Mixed-Dry
- Marine

7. Why do you need a map key to understand the climate map?

8. A. In which part of Canada do you think most people live? Why?
   B. How many different climates exist in the United States?
   C. Name two climate areas that most likely indicate a desert region.

9. What is the climate of the region you live in? Use the political map to estimate the location of your state on the climate map.

10. Describe how temperatures change from the northern regions to the southern regions of North America.

Compare and Contrast the two maps in terms of map features, information presented, intended purpose, and level of detail.

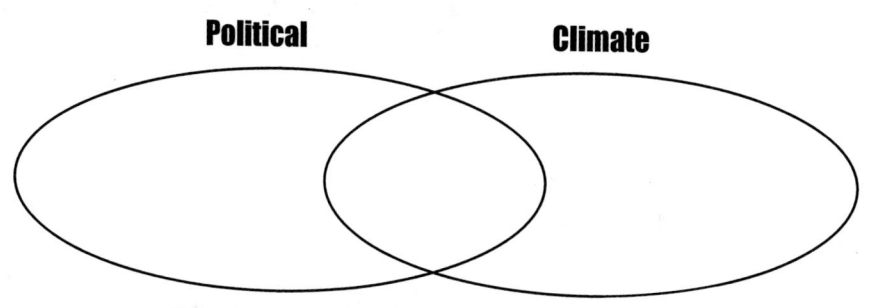

Political   **Climate**

©Carole Marsh/Gallopade • www.gallopade.com • page 19

COMPARISON OF SOURCES

Physical & Resource Maps

Look at the maps and complete Parts A, B, and C.

Physical maps illustrate the physical features of an area, such as mountains, deserts, rivers, oceans, and lakes. They can be used to view Earth's natural features, like landforms, bodies of water, and vegetation.

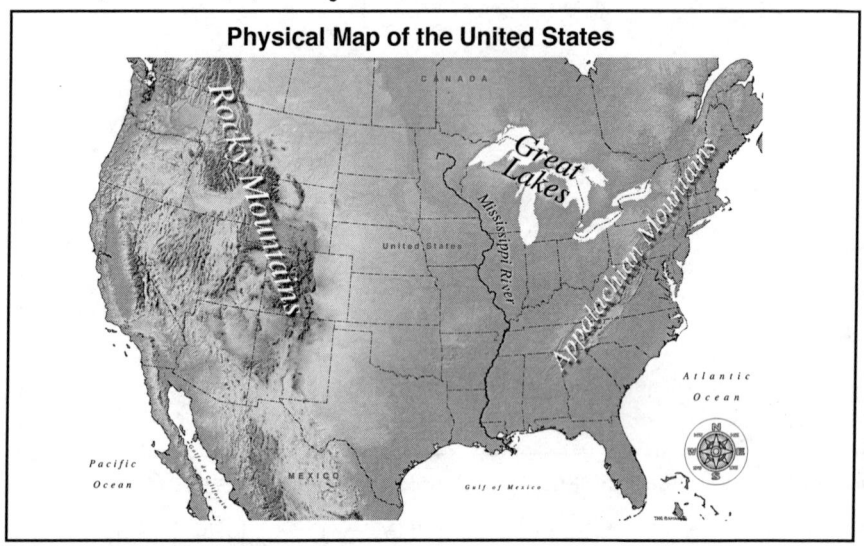

Physical Map of the United States

Economic and resource maps show the types of natural resources or economic activities that dominate an area.

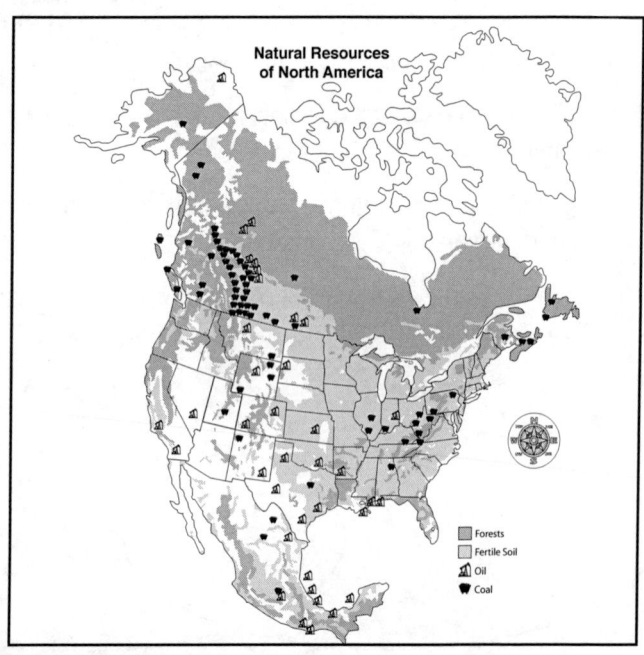

Natural Resources of North America

- Forests
- Fertile Soil
- Oil
- Coal

©Carole Marsh/Gallopade • www.gallopade.com • page 20

PART A: Look at the physical map and answer the questions.

1. What is the purpose of a physical map?
2. Explain why a physical map might be important to a:
   A. construction company   B. farmer   C. hiking enthusiast
3. What information can you gather from the title of this map?
4. A. What major landform is visible along the western part of North America?
   B. Find another example of that type of landform in the eastern U.S.
5. A. List at least 3 types of bodies of water shown on this map.
   B. List an example of each from the map.

PART B: Look at the resource map and answer the questions.

6. What is the purpose of a resource map?
7. Explain why a map key is necessary to read this resource map.
8. What political information is also included on this resource map?
9. A. List at least three products that you know are made from forests.
   B. Where in North America is there a large supply of forest resources?
10. Does this map represent all of the resources in North America? Support your answer with logical thinking

PART C: Consider information from both maps and answer these questions.

11. In the United States and Canada, coal is most commonly found near what natural landforms?
12. Many Midwestern states have strong agricultural industries.
    A. What natural resource supports agriculture in the Midwest?
    B. What major physical feature supports agriculture in the Midwest?
13. Is the Southwestern United States likely to have an industry based on agriculture? Cite evidence from the maps to explain why or why not.
14. How are natural resources affected by the physical features of the land? Cite evidence from the maps to support your conclusion.

©Carole Marsh/Gallopade • www.gallopade.com • page 21

GRAPHICAL DATA ANALYSIS
A Map Series

Look at the table and maps to answer the questions.

The table marks important events of westward expansion that resulted in land exchange between Native Americans and the United States.

Westward Expansion Event	Years
Trail of Tears	1838-1839
California Gold Rush	1849-1858
Transcontinental Railroad	1863
Indian Wars	1865-1890

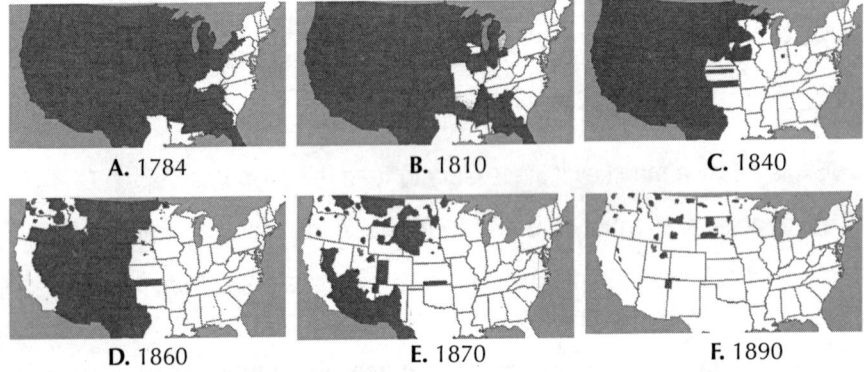

A. 1784   B. 1810   C. 1840

D. 1860   E. 1870   F. 1890

Dark areas = Native American Land   White areas = United States land

1. Write a descriptive title for the series of six maps.

2. How is the information in the table similar to the information presented on the maps? How is the information in the table different?

3. Place a ✓ next to the statement that best describes the purpose of this map series. Explain your choice.
   a) _____ compare land features of the U.S.
   b) _____ show change over time
   c) _____ explain why people moved west

4. A. In 1784, who occupied most of the land?
   B. In 1890, who occupied most of the land?

5. Which map best shows the direct effects of each of the following:
   A. Trail of Tears   C. Transcontinental Railroad
   B. California Gold Rush   D. Indian Wars

©Carole Marsh/Gallopade • www.gallopade.com • page 22

PRIMARY SOURCE ANALYSIS
Aerial Painting

Read the text and answer the questions.

Aerial paintings and photographs are a form of map because they show the Earth from above. Aerial paintings often show cities or battlefields and capture a period of history.

VIEW OF WASHINGTON CITY.

Courtesy of the Library of Congress

1. What do you notice first in the aerial painting? Make at least three other observations about the painting.

2. A. Locate the title of this aerial painting.
   B. What information does the title give you?
   C. What inferences can you make about the large building in the foreground?

3. A. Describe the layout of "Washington City."
   B. What famous landmark can you see in the background?

4. What evidence in the painting suggests that this painting was not created in the last 100 years?

5. Use an online resource to find a similar image of Washington, D.C. today. Describe how the city has changed, and identify the correct name of the building shown in this painting.

©Carole Marsh/Gallopade • www.gallopade.com • page 23

Correlations to Common Core State Standards

For your convenience, correlations are listed page-by-page, and for the entire book!

This book is correlated to the Common Core State Standards for English Language Arts grades 3-8, and to Common Core State Standards for Literacy in History, Science, & Technological Subjects grades 6-8.

Correlations are highlighted in gray.

PAGE #	READING Includes: RI: Reading Informational Text RH: Reading History/Social Studies	WRITING Includes: W: Writing WHST: Writing History/Social Studies, Science, & Technical Subjects	LANGUAGE Includes: L: Language LF: Language Foundational Skills	SPEAKING & LISTENING Includes: SL: Speaking & Listening
2	RI/RH . 1 2 3 4 5 6 7 8 9 10	W/WHST . 1 2 3 4 5 6 7 8 9 10	L/LF . 1 2 3 4 5 6	SL . 1 2 3 4 5 6
3	RI/RH . 1 2 3 4 5 6 7 8 9 10	W/WHST . 1 2 3 4 5 6 7 8 9 10	L/LF . 1 2 3 4 5 6	SL . 1 2 3 4 5 6
4-5	RI/RH . 1 2 3 4 5 6 7 8 9 10	W/WHST . 1 2 3 4 5 6 7 8 9 10	L/LF . 1 2 3 4 5 6	SL . 1 2 3 4 5 6
6-7	RI/RH . 1 2 3 4 5 6 7 8 9 10	W/WHST . 1 2 3 4 5 6 7 8 9 10	L/LF . 1 2 3 4 5 6	SL . 1 2 3 4 5 6
8-9	RI/RH . 1 2 3 4 5 6 7 8 9 10	W/WHST . 1 2 3 4 5 6 7 8 9 10	L/LF . 1 2 3 4 5 6	SL . 1 2 3 4 5 6
10	RI/RH . 1 2 3 4 5 6 7 8 9 10	W/WHST . 1 2 3 4 5 6 7 8 9 10	L/LF . 1 2 3 4 5 6	SL . 1 2 3 4 5 6
11	RI/RH . 1 2 3 4 5 6 7 8 9 10	W/WHST . 1 2 3 4 5 6 7 8 9 10	L/LF . 1 2 3 4 5 6	SL . 1 2 3 4 5 6
12-13	RI/RH . 1 2 3 4 5 6 7 8 9 10	W/WHST . 1 2 3 4 5 6 7 8 9 10	L/LF . 1 2 3 4 5 6	SL . 1 2 3 4 5 6
14-15	RI/RH . 1 2 3 4 5 6 7 8 9 10	W/WHST . 1 2 3 4 5 6 7 8 9 10	L/LF . 1 2 3 4 5 6	SL . 1 2 3 4 5 6
16-17	RI/RH . 1 2 3 4 5 6 7 8 9 10	W/WHST . 1 2 3 4 5 6 7 8 9 10	L/LF . 1 2 3 4 5 6	SL . 1 2 3 4 5 6
18-19	RI/RH . 1 2 3 4 5 6 7 8 9 10	W/WHST . 1 2 3 4 5 6 7 8 9 10	L/LF . 1 2 3 4 5 6	SL . 1 2 3 4 5 6
20-21	RI/RH . 1 2 3 4 5 6 7 8 9 10	W/WHST . 1 2 3 4 5 6 7 8 9 10	L/LF . 1 2 3 4 5 6	SL . 1 2 3 4 5 6
22	RI/RH . 1 2 3 4 5 6 7 8 9 10	W/WHST . 1 2 3 4 5 6 7 8 9 10	L/LF . 1 2 3 4 5 6	SL . 1 2 3 4 5 6
23	RI/RH . 1 2 3 4 5 6 7 8 9 10	W/WHST . 1 2 3 4 5 6 7 8 9 10	L/LF . 1 2 3 4 5 6	SL . 1 2 3 4 5 6
COMPLETE BOOK	RI/RH . 1 2 3 4 5 6 7 8 9 10	W/WHST . 1 2 3 4 5 6 7 8 9 10	L/LF . 1 2 3 4 5 6	SL . 1 2 3 4 5 6

For the complete Common Core standard identifier, combine your grade + "." + letter code above + "." + number code above.

In addition to the correlations indicated here, the activities may be adapted or expanded to align to additional standards and to meet the diverse needs of your unique students!

©Carole Marsh/Gallopade • www.gallopade.com • page 24